I0829755

Deep Wells, Reservoirs and Aquifers: Writing About Family

Jon Obermeyer

2023

In loving memory of
Dorothy Summers Bowers
(1902-2002)

Also by Jon Obermeyer

Poetry
The Reassurance of Ghosts

Salsipuedes

Occupational Hazards

Wingspan

Siren Call SF (images by Dwayne Newton)

The Principles of Composition

Your Mileage May Vary

Initiation: Nature Poems

Dissolve

Y Nada Mas: Poems for a Pandemic

Senior Housing

Transit Power

Memoir
It Happens That Fast

Briarcliff

The Harbor

The Guests

Fiction
The Winter Practice and Other Stories

Centripetal Force and Other Stories

Inflection Point: 18 Stories

Let's Not And Say We Did (Stories)

Essay
The Low Wire

Myriad: A Poet's Perspective on Writing

Laying Low

Writing Guides
Big Splash: Writing Your First Book

Likely Story: First-Time Fiction

Brought into Light: The Making of Memoir

Contents

Every tea-table is a battlefield,
littered with old catastrophes
and haunted by vague ghosts.

—W.H. Auden, *For the Time Being*

Modern writing manuals often conflate story with conflict.... Conflict is one kind of behavior. There are others, equally important in any human life, such as relating, finding, losing, bearing, discovering, parting, changing. Change is the universal aspect of all these sources of story. Story is something moving, something happening, something or somebody changing.

— Ursula K. Le Guin

Introduction: Happy Families

Happy families are all alike. They don't produce writers.

That epigraph is my twist on the famous Tolstoy quote, which referred to the uniqueness of Unhappy Families.

This book grew out of a 90-minute writing workshop that I led in 2016 for my friend Lori Hagberg's class of middle schoolers in Valencia, CA.

In 2018, I expanded this material for a North Carolina Writer Network workshop in Chapel Hill. Later that year, I developed it into a full day workshop and a five-week writing class for Central Carolina Community College in Pittsboro, North Carolina.

As I looked at my presentation deck of 30 slides for the workshop, I thought, "this is almost enough material for a book." Some of this material I had previously developed as a chapter in my poetry writing guide, Myriad (2017).

When you write about family, there is no limit to it and no limit to the ways of talking about it. You can write about your parents, your siblings, your aunts and uncles, your grandparents and their siblings, plus your own offspring. And then if you run out of material, you can start hacking away at the ancestral forest.

For example, I've written about my maternal grandmother, Dorothy, and several poems about my paternal grandfather Grey. I also have a book I want to write about my Irish great-great grandparents who emigrated from County Kerry to Manitoba, Canada after the potato famine in the 1840s.

I have a four book series underway about my great-great grandfather Capt. Ed Welty, who was a Union cavalry officer in the Civil War, an Indian Scout with Kit Carson and a Val-paraiso, Indiana newspaper publisher.

And when you have exhausted your family quarry, you can shift and write about your in-laws, or even have strangers like my former wife's elderly neighbor who flew for the Royal Air Force in World War II. He had a great anecdote about being served powdered eggs every morning that he didn't fly bombing missions, and when you were served real eggs, you knew you were going to fly that day.

Another variable for this topic involves genre. This guidebook is written for anybody who writes about family in poetry, memoir, fiction, or creative nonfiction.

This book is designed with a practical purpose in mind: that you actually write something. Start with something small (like an interesting character or family event that becomes the core of a larger piece. Eventually, the proverbial grain of sand inside the oyster leads to the pearl.

To that end, my instructional content in this book is balanced frequently with writing prompts and exercises. Use the white space wisely.

Writing about family is a noble if not ceremonial role. It's how oral history has occurred throughout the ages.

Writing is about authenticity. You want to figure out who you are at a certain deeper level by exploring your heritage, Or, you may be writing about your family as a less expensive alternative to months of therapy.

Whatever the motivation. I hope you find this writing guide entertaining, useful, and inspiring.

1
Deep Wells, Reservoirs and Aquifers

*I find the family to be the most mysterious and fascinating institu-
tion in the world*
— Amos Oz

For the poet, fiction writer and memoirist, family represents a
deep well of material, a vast reservoir with unlimited water,
or, if you consider families beside your own, it's a big, giant
freshwater aquifer like the State of Florida rests upon.

Families can be an endless source of characters, especially as
you move beyond parents and siblings into your larger family
tree. Adjacent family members like cousins, aunts and uncles
are especially interesting for a writer because of the arms-
length objectivity and the variant of your DNA combined with
that of a completely different family that you get with cousins.

Family dynamics abound as you trace relationships between
characters and the dramatic possibilities inherent in those
connections. There's also a rich trove of family lore, myth and
allegory to explore.

I'm thinking of my grandmother in Southern Alberta crossing
a high train trestle over the Little Bow River as she walked to
school in all sorts of weather. I'm remembering how my father
brought home a handwritten death threat he had received at
work from a member of the Mafia.

There are thousands if not millions of details once you tap into the family archives. Not just what people look like, but what they said or thought.

You have an option as a narrator or voice of the piece. Do you want to relate 100^ of the truth or do you want to take a creative leap into conjecture as you embellish the family anecdote with period research and your imagination?

I've always been intrigued by my maternal grandmother bringing home the body of my grandfather by train in 1964, after he had a heart attack while they were on vacation.

What was it like to have him pass away right in front of her, two states away from home in New Mexico? What was on her mind, as she passed through Arizona and back into California, riding in a passenger car while his body was in the freight car?

Since my grandmother is no longer alive, I have to imagine and embellish this tiny scrap of family lore that was related to me as a child.

Another fun exercise is mapping a family member's overlap with history. My paternal ancestor's house was occupied by the Confederate army during the Battle of Gettysburg. The house offered a strategic location as an observation post, overlooking the battlefield. My great-great-great grandmother would have most likely hosted and fed the Rebel soldiers, while hiding the fact that her son was a Union officer.

My great-great grandfather Ed Welty was a cavalry captain in the Civil War in charge of a hundred men in their horses in the Shenandoah Valley campaigns of 1863 to 1864. After mustering out in 1865, he rode around the west with Kit Carson joined Custer's Custer's seventh Cavalry, but got out long before Little Big Horn.

My great-uncle Charlie, a Detroit newspaper executive, negotiated Teamster's contracts with Jimmy Hoffa and was served a subpoena by Bobby Kennedy to testify about those quote business relationships before Congress.

My great grandfather, William Obermeyer, was a barber on the Super Chief train that ran between Los Angeles and Chicago. Near the end of his career, my great-grandfather gave a shave on the train to the syndicated columnist Ernie Pyle. Pyle wrote about that shave in a nationally-syndicated column. I wrote a poem based on that intersection, and this is just scratching the surface.

If you're stuck about what to write about next, consider a family member present or past. These stories surround you, just waiting to be told.

Exercise 1
Pick a Family Member, Any Family Member

The magician holds out the deck of cards and tells you to "pick a card. any card."

This apppears random, but the range of probability is actually quite narrow. There are only 52 possible cards that make up the deck, and there are only four suits. It's not as random as you might think.

Pick a family member, any family member, to be your main character or subject.

By selecting one family member, you may find it helpful to narrow your focus, choosing a family member worthy of characterization or commemoration in literary work, if only as the initial spark or basis for something else,

1. Write down the family member's name. i will refer to this character/family member throughout the book.

2. Write down why you picked that family member to write about. What makes them attractive or compelling is subject matter? Is this something specific or an overall sense?

3. Write down your preferred go-to genre: writing, poetry, fiction, creative essay or memoir.

2

Capturing Biographical Information and Observations

I have selected my maternal grandmother, Dorothy Summers Bowers (1902-2002), as my family member.

Why? She lived to be 100 years old She saw Halley's Comet twice in her lifetime and witnessed most of the 20th century.

I have some guilt about her passing, that I was not able to visit her during the last three years of her life or attend her funeral, but I have written about her in several poems, in my memoir It Happens That Fast, and in several short stories.

Here are 20 biographical facts and observations about my grandmother:

1. She was born in Chicago, Illinois in 1902.

2. A family illness led the family to move to Alberta, Canada.

3. They were the first settlers of the village of Carmangay,.

4. She spent her childhood in southern Alberta on the Canadian prairie with four siblings.

5. She was frugal, unflappable, and a strict Baptist, *brassbound* might say it best.

6. She loved birds.

7. She was very proper and an Anglophile. She loved the Commonwealth and its Queen.

8. She had unique terms for things, like "davenport" for sofa and "grip" for suitcase.

9. She witnessed Halley's Comet twice in her lifetime, in 1910 and in 1986.

10. She moved to Calgary after high school and met my grandfather, a native of Manitoba.

11. They married and immigrated to the US in 1928.

12. Two daughters were born, my mother in 1935 and my aunt in 1938.

13. She was a skier, an outdoors woman in Washington and Oregon.

14. She was a working mom. She was a bank teller and late in life, she worked in appliance sales.

15. She made her own dresses, using Butterick sewing patterns.

16. She moved with my grandfather to Southern California in 1953.

17. She became a widow in 1964 when her husband died suddenly on the first leg of a train trip around the U.S.

18. She later went around the United States, solo, on a Greyhound bus Ameripass.

19. She was a surrogate parent to me and my sister.

20. She took me traveling with her by train and bus throughout the United States, to the Grand Canyon, Yellowstone National Park and Seattle.

Exercise 2
Biographical Facts and Observations

Like I have demonstrated with my maternal grandmother, write down 20 biographical facts or observations about the family member that you selected an Exercise One.

These 20 biographical facts and observations could become the chapter titles and basis for an entire book. Any one of them might inspire a poem or a short story.

Hopefully, they will become the basis of even more curiosity about your family member, so that you will want to increase the overall number of facts or write more extensively about any one of them as journal entries, sketches or stories.

If there's an unknown detail on your list, flag it for further research, investigation or exploration with your imagination.

3

Understanding Happiness

Alvy Singer: You look like you're a very happy couple.
Female street stranger. Yeah.
Alvy Singer. Yeah. So how do you account for it?
Female Street Stranger. Um, I'm very shallow and empty and I have
no ideas and nothing interesting to say.
Male Streets Stranger: And I'm exactly the same way

In this classic scene from *Annie Hall* (1977), Woody Allen cleverly
equates happiness with shallowness. It's not worth his time. He
would rather be obsessing over death, his relationship with his new
girlfriend, Annie and her family, or, the main cultural advantage of
California, being able to turn right on red light.

Our human brain did not evolve to deal with happiness and har-
mony. The human prefrontal cortex is 200,000 years old, and it's
designed for risk mitigation, predator avoidance, and complex
socialization (with up to 125 of individuals in your extended family
and tribe).

According to the cognitive neuroscientist Dr. Michael Gazzaniga at
U.C. Santa Barbara, our brains manufacture a risk-mitigation form
of reality milliseconds ahead of actual events, in order to protect
us from harm. This allowed our ancestors to quickly distinguish
between a stick and a deadly snake on a jungle path. So ultimately,
everything is fiction.

If I ask you to write about what happened to you an hour ago or earlier today, it will not be completely accurate. You will omit some details, or you'll cloud what you tell me by adding bias, opinion and hindsight.

I hope this frees you to write as fully as you can to render a scene or backstory about your family member without worrying if you got it exactly right. If what you write is dark and troubled, there might be a good reason for it. Happiness is a fiction, and not very useful to evolutionary biology.

Exercise 3
Exploring Happiness

Is it possible to write about happiness in families? If so, would readers find that interesting?

Can you find a way to make happiness interesting as a writer?

What other ways can you approach happiness in your story about your family member?

You could write about the "calm before the storm," the happiness that precedes a dark period or devastating event

You could create a happy ending to that dark period or devastating event.

You could write about a character who exudes happiness, is happy on the surface, but hides troubled memories.

You could write about someone who finds a "happy medium," balancing lightness and darkness, with neither extreme highs or lows. In World War II, soldiers in the Pacific invented a term called "rock happy," which referred to becoming mentally unstable after spending too much time on one island.

As much as there is conflict in families, see if you can weave an element of happiness into your character development and story.

4
Five Film Families

I'm a film nut, especially when it comes to independent films like Junebug and Juno. These are the types of films that Richard Gere (Norman) recently described as "the kinds of studio movies the studios used to make."

I've selected five movies based on the storytelling complexity, sophisticated character development and family dynamics portrayed.

They're all worth watching, and rewatching, like a writer, not a spectator. Pay attention to how the characters are developed and the story is constructed:

Rushmore (1998) is about a father and his son, but also a father and his sons.

Magnolia (1999) is about fathers and sons, and a father-daughter dynamic.

August. Osage County (2013 is about siblings, originally a Tracy Letts play

Fences (2016), is about a father and son dynamic, originally in August Wilson play.

Toni Erdmann (2016) is about a father daughter dynamic.

5
Family as Kindling for the Fire

Sometimes I get the start of a story from a memory or an anecdote,
but that gets lost and is usually unrecognizable in the final story.
— Alice Munro

Attach your family history onto something larger that is happening
at the time. (the Irish famine, women suffrage, religious movements).
If you get something like that, then you've got the book.
— William Maxwell

Part of the new book is about my family for material that I have
gleaned from research, and part of it is from my own life and my own
experience, but not always completely autobiographical, completely
based on fact. Some of these stories have fictional elements to them,
but they're almost very psychologically true.
— Alice Munro

6

The Family in Short Fiction

The short story form is ideal for exploring family relationships. Short stories are concise, compact, and potentially lyrical. Short fiction is a crucible where art is formed.

In the early 1990s, I wrote a short story called "The Mystery of My Mother," which was later published in the anthology O.Henry Festival Stories.

It is not a story about my mother. It is written from the first-person point-of-view of my former wife. It is a fictional story about her relationship with her mother, my mother-in-law.

The story was inspired by a funeral I attended one cold winter day with my wife and my mother-in-law. The funeral was for my mother-in-law's boyfriend, who had died of cancer.

To my mother-in-law's dismay, the boyfriend's ex-wife was awarded a front row seat and my mother-in-law was left out in the cold, i.e. seated in the back row of the funeral home.

A further complication to this comical day involved a stop for hot cocoa on the way to the cemetery and arriving at the grave site far in advance of the funeral procession. I also remember that the boyfriend's grave site was the furthest possible plot away from the road, and that the casket was extremely heavy (I was a last minute pallbearer).

I used that funeral as a jumping off point for my former wife to explore her complicated, often comical, relationship with her mother, which was also a way for me to understand my mother-in-law who'd been a surrogate parent for me when I was in my mid twenties.

I also knew from family lore that there had been an earlier funeral when my mother-in-law was a teenager and her mother had passed away. I realized the two funerals were connected and soon my story was underway. Most of the events in my story are loosely based on real events and I used my imagination to fill in the gaps and created a unique, entertaining work of fiction.

Below is a list of short stories by writers who draw heavily on the family as a source for their fiction. Pay particular attention to the main family dynamic (fathers and sons in Ford and Hemingway, mothers and sons in Updike). Make sure you capture something of that connection in your work.

Any short story by Alice Munro.

Any short story by William Trevor.

Rock Springs, Richard Ford (1987)

The Nick Adams Stories, Ernest Hemingway (1972)

"Good Country People," "A Good Man is Hard to Find," and "A Late Encounter with the Enemy" by Flannery O'Connor.

"Down at the Dinghy," "Teddy," "Just Before the War with the Eskimos" by Jerome David Salinger.

"Flight" and "Friends from Philadelphia" by John Updike

"Everyday Use" by Alice Walker

Exercise 4
The Family in Short Fiction

Read any short story listed in chapter 6 or reread your favorite short story that has a strong family element to it.

Why do you like the story?

Is there anything in the story similar to something that happened in your family?

Write a 1,500-word (six-page) short-short story based on your family member? Use one of tjhe biographical details from Exercise 2 to get you started.

I've written a 1,000-word short story called "Trestle," based on my grandmother Dorothy's childhood in southern Alberta, growing up on the Canadian prairie with four siblings. I knew from family lore that the five kids had to walk across a very high railroad trestle to get to school, and sometimes a freight train would come along when they were only halfway across the trestle.

7
The Family in Novels

The novel form allows the writer to write expansively in great detail, and in large, sweeping themes that span entire decades (Buddenbrooks) or capture a single day (Ulysses).

In Thomas Mann's 1901 novel *Buddenbrooks*, he uses the novel format to examine several generations of one family. Three of the novels below (Potok, Steinbeck, and Bellow), feature a strong father-son dynamic. Waugh's novel is about a mother holds undue sway over her son and ultimately ruins him.

This is not an exclusive list of family themed novels, but merely a curation of several titles worth considering for this genre.

Buddenbrooks, Thomas Mann

My Name is Asher Lev, Chaim Potok

East of Eden. John Steinbeck

Seize the Day, Saul Bellow

Brideshead Revisited, Evelyn Waugh

The Corrections, Jonathan Franz

My Dream of You, Nuala O'Faolain

Exercise 5
Character Development

Take your selected family member from Exercise One and map
them to two or three other family members. Connect Aunt
Edith to Uncle Charlie. Now, connect Aunt Edith to her
husband Albee. Make another connection to their children,
your cousins.

I happen to be close to my mom's sister, Roberta in the same
way. My dad was close to his Aunt Lela, also known as "Aunt
Sis," my grandfather's sister.

I have found that aunts tend to be very protective of their
nephews. They nurture them and have a special fondness. I
am also close to my dad's late sister Frances Miller, who was a
talented painter. We have a bond of creativity between us in a
way that her three sons, my cousins, don't have.

There is a clarity to a nephew-aunt or niece-uncle relationship
that can produce a closeness not even found between parent
and child. I sense that my parents' siblings have some secret
perspective or insight that will help me understand my mom
or my dad.

On the connecting lines of your diagram, label the
psychological dynamic between the family members, love,
anger, redemption, irritation.

Next, write down three interesting details about the related family member.

What is something about this family member that you've wondered about?

Are you comfortable making up the gaps with imagination or conjecture?

Finally, what genre will best tell his or her story?

8
Family Dynamics

Families are good for exploring complex interrelationships between characters. Try to find the spark and tension between two or more characters.

Think of the relationship between the two sets of brothers in Steinbeck's novel, *East of Eden*: Adam and Charles Trask in post-Civil War Connecticut, and Adam's twin sons, Aaron and Caleb in the pre-World War I Salinas Valley of California.

The Aaron - Caleb dynamic echoes the Cane - Abel rivalry from the Old Testament. The Hamilton family in the novel is based on the real life family of Samuel Hamilton, Steinbeck's maternal grandfather.

There's quite a bit written these days about sibling birth order. If you're going to have siblings as characters in a work of fiction or subject matter for a memoir or a poem, you might want to look at birth order dynamics to give you more insight into your characters and why they behave the way they do.

9
Family Lore and Myth

Every family has some kind of lore that they refer to on
occasion. Sometimes you hear about it around the dinner table
and sometimes it will surface at a family reunion.

For my parents, the lore was how poor they were when they
were first married in the early 1960's, and how with their last
two quarters on a Sunday afternoon, they took me to ride the
miniature train in Griffith Park in Los Angeles.

My grandmother Dorothy talked about seeing Halley's Comet
for the first time in the Alberta Prairie in 1910, without any
light pollution from surrounding cities.

She lived long enough to see it again in Southern California in
1986, but I don't believe it was the same experience as seeing it
as an eight-year-old in the vast night sky above Alberta.

That same grandmother also told us about having to walk
over a high railroad trestle above the Little Bow River with her
siblings on the way to school, which I wrote about in the short
story "Ttrestle."

If a freight train came along, there wasn't time to get off the
trestle, and so there were wooden boxes with lids built into the
side of the trestle for the children to take shelter.

When I saw the Terrence Malick film *Days of Heaven* in 1978,
I felt an immediate affinity with the stunning landscapes and
backdrops of the ocean-like expanse of wheat fields.

Although Malik's fictional story is set in the Texas Panhandle,
I found out later it was filmed in the same part of Southern
Alberta where my grandmother grew up. The family lore
became intensely real for me.

10
Drama/Comedy/Tragedy

The family provides all three of the traditional elements that you will need to tell your story. You just have to go back and identify what they might be.

We categorize our movies these days as thrillers, rom-coms and documentaries.

What kind of family story do you have in front of you?

Do what you can to play against type, to shift and reassemble the elements of the family story artistically.

If your story is a drama, lighten it with comedic interludes and light moments.

If it's a farce or comedy, give it some dark edges.

In the theater, *The Merchant of Venice* and *The Winter's Tale* by William Shakespeare, *The Cherry Orchard* by Anton Chekhov, and *The Caretaker* by Harold Pinter, are all considered tragi-comedies.

In fiction, *Candide* by Voltaire, *A Handful of Dust* by Evelyn Waugh and *Catch-22* by Joseph Heller are also considered tragicomedy. Anything by Southern Gothic writer Flannery O'Connor fits the category.

11

Children and Grandchildren Count as Family

Writing About Family not only includes your grandparents and ancestors. Children and grandchildren count also.

You can write to your children, but you can also write about your children.

In March, 2018, I wrote a short, 68-page memoir titled *Briarcliff*, which was the name of the street we lived on in Greensboro, North Carolina when my daughter Katherine was young.

The memoir covers the years 1985-1993, and covers a period of time several years before my daughter's arrival when we lived in the Latham Park neighborhood. The two-story brick Cape Cod house, with round dormers upstairs, happened to have been built by my former wife's grandparents, so we had a real connection to family history living there.

Briarcliff covers Katherine's first four years of life, including 1989 when Hurricane Hugo slammed into Charleston, South Carolina as a Category-Five hurricane, and traveled 200 miles inland to cause destruction in Charlotte and Greensboro. 1989 was also the year of the Tiananmen Square protests and massacre and the fall of the Berlin Wall, so a momentous arrival by my daughter.

I wrote *Briarcliff* for my Katherine's 29th birthday, in May of that year.

Not to be outdone, her younger sister Liz, who has a June birthday, said to me, "what the heck, Dad, where's my book?"

Out of that question, I wrote *The Harbor: An Era of Innocence Before 9/11* for Liz, which covers the first eight years of her life.

Here's another suggestion. Write a children's book for your child or grandchild.

12
Millions of Details (all senses)

From the 1500's through the year 1800, life expectancy in Europe was around 30 to 40 years. Life expectancy doubled over the next ten generations, thanks to improved health care, sanitation, immunizations, access to clean running water, and better nutrition. Now we live into our 80's and 90's.

If you live to be 80 years old, that means you are around for 29,200 days. That's a lot of living.

Out of all those years, you should be able to mine thousands, if not millions, of details:

The clothes, shoes and jewelry they wore.

The cars they drove, or earlier in time, the horses they rode

The foods they raised, prepared and consumed.

The weather they endured.

The economic cycles they experienced, the recessions and the booms, the good times and the bad.

As a writer, you should be constantly collecting the sights, smells, and tastes of whatever era you have chosen. You can either uncover these details through research, or invent them using your imagination.

13

Narrator/Monologue (Point of View)

You have a choice in fiction and poetry.

Instead of telling your main character's story using a third-person point-of-view (third-person limited or omniscient), consider having your family member narrate the story in the first-person.

Take the Great Depression (1929-1939).

How was that event viewed by my grandfather, who was in his thirties or my great-grandfather in his sixties?

My grandfather Grey would've been in his prime, working years, responsible for a wife and two children.

My great-grandfather Wi,iam would've been on the verge of retirement, his children already the house with children of their own. Another kind of worrying concern.

What was my mother's take on World War II food rationing when she was a young girl growing up in Seattle?

What was it like knowing that Japanese submarines had entered Puget Sound and the far off war from the newsreels was very much a part of daily life?

For me, The first-person point-of-view provides a hands-on immediacy, where you channel the actual speaking voice and perspective of your family member. This strategy is a terrific way to "get into character" and into the mind of your subject, much like an actor completely takes on a role.

I prefer this approach to the detached, hands-off, third-person point-of-view when looking to delve deeply into a story.

14
Dialogue and Dialect

Many of us come from immigrant families, whether they arrived from Europe, Mexico, Asia, or Eastern Europe.

What language did your ancestors or family members speak, growing up?

Growing up in upstate New York, my grandfather Grey spoke German in the house until age six, which also meant he probably spoke his first English in school with a German accent.

What is it like for the children of immigrants to learn and speak perfect English because of school and peer pressure, while their parents still speak with an accent and are slower to assimilate?

Use this dichotomy to enrich your work.

As a fun exercise, write two pages of dialogue between your main character and another family member. See if you can create the rhythm and cadence of speech that sounds like regular speech.

15
Plot

"The king died, and then the queen died" is a story, while "The king died, and then the queen died of grief," is a plot.
— E.M. Forster

What will be the structure of your work, especially a work of fiction? Is there a narrative arc?

The plot is the sequence of events in which each event affects the next one through the principle of cause-and-effect.

Often your family history or lore can help guide you, with some natural plotting based on facts (even if you're writing a work of fiction). Occasionally, the facts will only take you so far. You may have to resort to leaps of imagination to cover the gaps and interpret the unknowns.

Sometimes your family history overlaps with actual history and you can draw on material already written about the larger events to inform your personal story.

For example, as I write about my great-great-grandfather Welty, the Union Army cavalry captain, the entire body of Civil War material (regimental histories, historical accounts, biographies, documentaries, soldier diaries and letters, newspaper accounts and photographs), is at my disposal as I create a work of fiction.

Exercise 6: Family Events

Below you'll find 14 transformative events which affect all families eventually.

Pick three or four events or circumstances that you would like to focus on in your work of fiction or your memoir. For a poem you might just want to focus on one element:

1. Death

2. Illness (debilitating or terminal)

3. Courtships and weddings (troubled marriages, affairs)

4. Divorce and remarriage, and the step-family dynamic,

5. Financial ruin and decline in social status,

6. Injustice

7. Adversity (financial, war, natural disasters)

8. Migration and immigration

9. Births, legitimacy, sibling rivalry and sibling warfare,

10. Discrimination (racism, sexism, ageism)

11. Mental illness

12. Abuse

13. Addiction

14. Malfeasance and crime.

Take a paragraph and describe how you'll weave each element into your work. Start writing down the supporting deals in bullet form. Go as deep as you possibly can. Add supporting details.

If there was mental illness in your family, what kind of mental illness? Was it undiagnosed or diagnosed? Was any kind of therapy or medication involved?

Did the mental illness result in any kind of harm or self-harm, including suicide or suicide attempt? Do you know the original cause of the mental illness? How far into the past do you need to go to find the source?

Did this mental illness manifest itself in future generations?

Did this mental illness have any redeeming qualities for that person or your family? Has there been a silver lining?

16
Nine Family Considerations

When writing about family, it's a fine line. You have to balance between creating truth and your literary artistry while not damaging your relationship with your subject matter.

If you choose to write about one of your ancestors, you might tick off one of the descendants who might not view the same story the same way you do.

Writing about family can be like walking through a minefield. Here are a few navigation and safety tips.

Consideration Number One: Permission.

If your family member is living, will you need to ask permission to write about them, or should you just plow ahead and ask for forgiveness later?

Some writers prefer to wait until the family member passes away before they write about them. I can't afford that "wait and write" strategy. If this person is important to my story, I need to write about them.

They may not like what I've written, but I'm more committed to my art than I am to my family members. It's a risk worth taking.

I may lose out on invitation to a future Thanksgiving, but I'm not going to ask for permission. It's not always an easy decision. You'll have to make your own choice about handling this one.

Consideration Number Two: Privacy

What if your subject claims you've violated their privacy?

First of all, I don't find the right to privacy anywhere in the constitution. Our founding fathers were not authors or publishers in a formal sense. What I see are the words "life, liberty, and the pursuit of happiness." Writing a story is my happiness, and I plan to pursue it.

Plus, in our social media world, what is privacy anyway, so many people put their lives out there in the public.

I'm not sure how much you can hide anyway. What I will do as a writer is respect your integrity. I will tell the story with as much truth as I can and make it authentic.

Let's say my grandfather was a bootlegger in the early 1920s. First off, that's fascinating copy. And if I know that Gramps made sour mash in a copper still and drove it down the mountain in a souped-up Chevy. I'm sure that other people are aware of that fact, especially as customers and the revenuers.

It's not like bootlegging is immoral. It was merely illegal during a certain period of time due to Prohibition, and maybe Gramps was doing the best he could to put food on the table and support his family. To me, that shows character.

"Gramps, what was it like? How did you pull it off?"

Consideration Number Three: Out in the Open

I would also look at the motivation of the writer and the mode
of publication.

Is the novel, memoir or poem about a family member
designed for private distribution and consumption, or will
it be published eventually and appear in the public domain?
Does the author have an agent and a publisher lined up,
especially a publisher with a huge marketing budget? Most
publishers do not have the budget to support a first-time
author with a tremendous amount of publicity.

Most literary works published in literary journals and in small
presses have very limited circulation. It's not like millions of
people will be reading this story.

Many literary works exist in backwater obscurity, while even
fewer publications are discovered and turned into screenplays
to become blockbuster films.

If a work is self-published, it's highly unlikely that many
people read it anyway, no more than 100 readers.

This should give you some level of comfort if the subject or
subject matter is controversial.

Consideration Number Four: Fact Checking

If you are writing a novel, fact checking doesn't really matter. You have created a work of fiction and will most likely have a disclaimer at the beginning of the book that states this. I would say the same thing for memoir, which falls into the category of "creative non-fiction."

Unless you're writing a straight-up biography, you shouldn't worry too much about fact checking. You are the writer. You own the facts.

When writing my memoir, *It Happens That Fast*, I did check on a few details with my cousin Lana for some tricky passages in a chapter about our maternal grandmother. Dorothy.

There are several trips that Lana and I both took with our grandmother and I wanted her take on my recollection, not just accuracy, but tone. Did I get it right? Does it feel the way you remember it?

In another chapter, I wanted to get the names correct for some of the more interesting teachers at Santa Barbara High School. I no longer have copies of my high school yearbook, so I went online to the "Damn Right, I Grew Up in Santa Barbara" Facebook site, which has 15,000 members. I could not remember the queries about the name of the toga-wearing football coach who also taught Roman history. His name was Mr. Everett, a name I couldn't track down anywhere.

Family Consideration Number Five: Masking

Even in nonfiction, you can mask your family members by changing their names, place, names and events. Yet anyone with a family knowledge or relationship is going to connect the dots.

Another strategy is to create an amalgam, a weaving together of several people in this single character or to create a single fictional character based on a real personage.

Another masking trick involves rejiggering the chronology or actually order of events in order to distance your story from the actual story.

I believe that ultimately the masking will fail you, and in the end, they're not all that necessary. Tell the story you need to tell.

Family Consideration Number Six: Author Bias

What I'm most careful about as a writer is my own bias and lens of looking at family members and events.

Do I have a chip on my shoulder about Uncle Ernie? Do I have an ax to grind about Cousin Willie?

Am I using my family story to air my grievance and get back at family members who have wronged me?

Memoir can be an inexpensive form of therapy and takes a lot less time on the couch with an analyst. In my memoir *It Happens That Fast.* I decided to go light around my parents and forgive some things I think they had no control over.

I was more interested in telling a true Santa Barbara story than I was hanging my parents out to twist in the wind.

When I addressed childhood depression, I did so in a way to show how any early hyper-sensitivity of my personality has actually benefited me later in life.

As an author and a parent to my own children, while there might have been emotional damage in my childhood, whatever happened has possibly made me a more compassionate friend and nurturing parent. After all, the word "depression," translated into German can mean "the courage to be heavy." It's a positive trait.

With all the emotional intelligence I can summon, I refuse to blame my parents for any negative environment in childhood. I'm going to thank them on paper, at least. Writing that memoir was a way of making peace with my past.

Family Consideration Seven: No-fly Zones.

Not all subjects are fair game for fiction and memoir or even a poem.

If you're dealing with incest, illegitimacy, or childhood abuse of any kind, I would urge you to tread lightly.

I have several topics I'm holding back on addressing in fiction or memoir, even though the family member I write about has already passed. I'm not sure I could handle the subject matter in anything more than a sensational manner.

For now, that story remains in the vault, on the back burner.

Family Consideration Eight: Burning Bridges

Writing about your family could have irrevocable consequences.

If you don't ask for permission and skirt the edges of personal privacy, you may pull it off in your current work, but it may affect future works.

Will your family sources clam up or want to be paid for anecdotes in the future?

Will Aunt Ethel want to share the royalties or points on the back end next time?

Will Uncle Ned write you out of his will because you wrote about his Korean War experience without permission?

Family Consideration Nine: Trust Your Instincts

Ultimately, your art requires authenticity and truth.

This is often a lonely road. You might have to say things in related events that are not pleasant for living family members or if they have passed, for their descendants.

You might have a glass of wine or ice water thrown in your face at the next family gathering, but if you told the story you are supposed to tell, it just might be worth the dry cleaning bill.

Plus, anyone who responds to me that vehemently immediately becomes an interesting character in my next book. Now, they are on my narrative radar.

Why did they react so strongly? What are they hiding? I'll have to look into this….

17

Are You Stuck? Borrow From Other Families

Sometimes you will exhaust the family material you have on hand.

As a writer, you have to be resourceful. Luckily, the world (i.e. the Internet) is here to help you. Below you'll find an inexhaustible list of go-to material, most of it in the public domain and not subject to copyright law.

From a legal interpretation, anything written before 1922 is considered public domain and subject to fair use. For anything written after 1922, be careful.

Unless you happen to write a blockbuster and land a mainstream publisher, nobody's gonna come after you.

I'm not saying you should plagiarize the work of other authors.

I'm mostly providing these ideas to help you become unstuck in your writing. Cite sparingly and use these resources as supplementary material.

Number One: Families in Scripture. Myth and Literature

The family has been around for a long time as fodder for
literary work. Most of the scripture of world religions has a
family dynamic to it and includes mythology and folklore.

Now add Shakespeare, Thomas Hardy Dickens Tolstoy, and
the works of George Elliot. If you can't find the family
structure you need in the vast library of world literature, I
would say you are not using your imagination to its fullest
potential.

Number Two: Newspapers

Your daily newspaper (and its online equivalent), is full of
family stories, especially in the obituary section.

Stay away from state and national news. Focus on the metro
section, and on feature stories, as they contain an immense
amount of background information and detail that could be
the inspiration for writing a novel or a memoir.

My high school friend Matt Soergel, is a an award-winning
features writer at the *Times-Union* in Jacksonville, Florida. He
has an knack for sniffing out any good story that comes across
his desk. It's like he has a special built-in radar that knows
how to find gold in the events and characters of Duval County,
in northeast Florida.

Number Three: Public Records, Private Papers

By law, our society maintains public records, including our court system and immigration records. There are public records of every commercial transaction. The military keeps records of every battle, minor skirmish and engagement.

On the private side, the church has always served as a keeper of records.

You should be able to find all kinds of family ideas and stories from the mundane recording of ordinary events for legal purposes, or from private papers.

Museums and libraries maintain special collections of letters and personal artifacts. They are not only authenticated, they're catalogued and preserved. For historical research, you might have to wear white gloves while you read them, but there are millions of private items available to you, all of them filled with family information.

It will be up to you to know what to do with all this information and how you'll weave it into your story.

Number Four: Museums

Every town has a museum. There are 35,000 museums in the United States, including the Antique Tractor Club in Greenwood, Delaware. The Forest Fire Museum in Moscow, Idaho, the Underground Salt Museum in Hutchinson, Kansas, the Museum of Maritime Pets in Indianapolis, Maryland, and the Museum of Bad Art in Somerville, Massachusetts.

Greensboro, North Carolina (population 200,000) has a Civil Rights museum. And three hours down the road in Bailey, North Carolina (population 563), you will find the Country Doctor Museum.

According to Wikipedia, 37 countries have Holocaust museums as well as 29 states in our country alone.

The folks at the museum in Porter County, Indiana have placed 1,300 transcribed biographies online, including one for my great-grandfather, Ed Welty, a captain in the Pennsylvania 14th Cavalry.

And from that brief biography, I was able to look up his regimental history online. From that regimental history, I found a list of over a hundred engagements from his cavalry unit, and several of these engagements have lengthy write-ups on Wikipedia. I can dive as deep as I want to on his military experience, just from free online documents.

Number Five: Heritage and Historical-Themed Associations

Don't forget the organizations that have been formed in honor
of our ancestors who fought in wars, the United Daughters of
the Confederacy and the Daughters of the American
Revolution.

If you're writing about the Korean or Vietnam Wars, a visit to a
local VFW post might be in order. Sadly, most of the surviving
veterans of World War II are in their nineties or have already
passed away. If you have a veteran in the family, interview
them now.

Number Six: For-profit Genealogy Sites

Sites like ancestry.com or Rich in Family History and Heritage, but may involve subscription or membership fees. These sites will mostly provide family names, dates, and locations from the census date, and you'll have to jump from then to the rich Resource Research resources above eight interviews.

Number Seven: Primary Research

There's nothing like conducting primary research.

I have found that neighbors, or even my friend's parents and relatives are willing subjects, especially on background, where their privacy will be protected. Most of them are delighted to share stories that their own kids don't want to hear anymore.

Another easy way to accomplish this is to visit your local Hardee's or McDonald's on the weekday morning and look for the group of white-haired gentlemen gathered in the corner. Most of them are likely talking about the good old days.

Be bold, jump in and start asking questions.

18
Memoir

History is written by the victors, but the victims write the memoirs
— Carol Tavris

Memoir is an ideal genre for writing about your family. All the
garden tools and nuclear warheads of creative non-fiction are
at your disposal. Tell the truth and then use your imagination
to fill in the gaps. Blur the lines if you have to.

Liars Club (1995) by Mary Karr and *Angela's Ashes* (1996) by
Frank McCourt were the first two of the breakthrough
memoirs of our time. Now it's a pandemic.

Richard Russo's *Elsewhere* (2012) is a memoir about the
writer's complicated relationship with his mother, and how
those complications lead to him being a better writer.

Richard Ford writes about both his parents in *Between Them*
(2017). Ford focuses on each parent separately, so in a way it's
like reading two memoirs.

I think very highly of William Finnegan's surfing memoir *A
Surfing Life*.

I'd also look at "My Father's Body at Rest and in Motion," an
essay by Siddhartha Muji in The New Yorker, January 8, 2018.

Exercise 7: Family Memoir

A memoir can be a combination of your personal story and the influence of another individual or individuals.

Start with your selected family member and outline a full table of contents for a family memoir. See if you can come up with at least 25 or 30 chapters on a first pass.

For a full memoir of 200 pages, you'll need at least 40 chapters averaging four or five pages each.

You can arrange the chapters chronologically or organize them under a common theme. The material itself should give you a strong infor indication of the structure.

Next, write a one-paragraph summary of each chapter, or if it's easier, write down four to five bullet points under each chapter title. Think of this as outlining each chapter.

Just for fun, write an informal three-page introduction to the memoir. Why did you write it? Who will benefit from reading it? Why are you the best one to tell a story?

19
The Family in Poetry

Think of a poem as a one-page, mini-memoir with line breaks.

I consider my debut poetry collection *The Reassurance of Ghosts* (2016) as 170- page memoir. The first third of the book covers 45 poems written from 1977-2009, the second third covers a prolific period of 55 poems written from 2010-2012 and the third section includes 38 poems witten about San Francisco, where I lived from 2013-2016.

While I was writing my memoir, *It Happens That Fast*, a flood of new poems emerged as I explored my Santa Barbara childhood. These new poems became part of my second poetry collection, *Salsipuedes*, in 2017.

I write about my family frequently in poems (see "1957")

Another poet who does this superbly is the late Philip Levine, a former U.S. poet laureate. This is why I included six poems from him below.

I find that reading a poem written by someone else can inspire a poem of my own. Sometimes it's just a single word or phrase that sparks my own memory, and then I'm off to the races. In the end, my poem has nothing at all to do with the poem that inspired it.

For family poems, I suggest reading:

"One Sister Have I in Our House," by Emily Dickinson,

"Kin" by Maya Angelou, and

"Zaydie," "Goodbye Uncle," "You Can Have It," "The New World,""The Return" and "More Than You Gave," by Philip Levine.

Exercise 8: Poetry

Write a poem from your family member's point-of-view, as a message to you, as if they are writing a letter to you.

Explore their relationship to you and imagine what they would say to you.

You can choose three different times to set the poem:

* They're writing in the poem to you when you were born.

* They're writing the poem to you when you were 19 years old

* They're writing to you at your current age.

20

Poems Based on Family Photographs

We capture family life in photographs. Here are three
examples of the poems-based-on-photographs sub-genre:

"From A Photograph" by George Oppen

"Sad Girl, Sitting on a Running Board" by Michael McFee.

"This is a Photograph of Me" by Margaret Atwood.

I will include my poem "1957" in this grouping:

1957
When California had yellow license plates,
the yearbook shows my dad with a crew cut
and black sneakers, poised at the starting line
for a college track meet.

There is a Kodachrome slide of my mother
in a turquoise sweater with round pearl buttons
illuminated by sunset and honeymoon,
her face is a reflection of candle glow.

Anyway, the starter's gun goes off,
the slide quickly drops
and the first born comes on the screen.
It happens that fast.

Exercise 9: Family Photograph Poems

Write a poem based on a family photograph.

Here are some questions to help you figure out what to write about:

Who took the picture?

What feeling or emotion is evoked by the scene? Joy, melancholy, unconditional love?

Can you tell the time of day or time of year?

Are there elements that transcend time?

Is there a sound or noise the photo makes?

Describe any smell. Are there particular aromas? Describe them.

Is your sense of taste activated by the photo?

Exercise 10: The Ross White Prompt

Ross White is a poet and teacher who lives in Durham, North Carolina. Ross came up with a great prompt writing prompt that I use repeatedly.

Take the favorite saying of a family member and tease it out as a story, poem or memoir.

Me: "Dad, can we go play basketball?"

Dad: "Let's not and say we did."

My Dad's saying is funny, but also kind of cruel and a blow-off to my question.

Here's another favorite saying of my parents:

Me: "I can't find my transistor radio."

Parents: "That's a shame. We paid good money for that."

This saying of my parents reflects a childhood upbringing during the Great Depresssion, when spending cash on non-essentials involved a different class of money, this so called "good money."

My mom did not just have a regular headache, she had a "splitting headache," which is quite gruesome when you actually picture it.

In the South, they say "how nice." which is not really meant to be a compliment.

"You have a new car, how nice." Can you hear the malice in how that is uttered?

Write down a list of three or four common sayings in your family, and then write a poem, short story or memoir chapter using that phrase as the title.

Let's Not Say and We Did

What parents say in passing
sticks, a barnacle on the hull
recalled at age fifty-eight
with a bit of bewilderment.

What did my dad mean
when he said "let's not?"
Did he not like me
putting him on the spot?
Was there a lawn that needed
mowing more than I needed
a pony ride? Was there old oil
in the Oldsmobile taking precedence
over my plea for hot beach sand?

Now that he's passed, I think
of the things we actually did:
Dodger Stadium, surf trips
to La Jolla, hikes to a waterfall.

He was barely out of adolescence,
a new parent fixing milkshakes
flipping char-grilled burgers
and making milk shakes
with a bachelor's degree.

I blame Herb Alpert.
I blame the Sixties
and the frenetic
unraveling that followed
my dad's Fu Manchu-
free spirit, sparring
with a need to salary.

I wear his sarcasm now
like a treasured Hang Ten shirt.
His reticence as essential armor.
I take into battle shielding me.

Exercise 11: Family Secrets

Every family has at least one secret. Some families have many hidden secrets, which is good if you're a writer.

Pick a family secret and write a two-page (500-word) short story or memoir chapter about it, or a poem, if you prefer.

Add as much detail as possible, and if you run out of facts, let your imagination kick in to fill the gaps. As you write about it, re-examine the severity of the secret. Is it all that bad? Has the passage of time taken the edge off? If you know about it, is it really secret?

If possible, see if you can interview the person who caused the situation that has been kept secret, or any family members who might have been affected by it, using your writing skill to make the secret interesting. Raise it above a cliche.

For example, I know of a family where one of the family members has been arrested several times, for the same offense. For some reason, this family member has not served any prison time but did spend one night in jail until bail was posted. Because of the arrests, this person has lost their job repeatedly, and in one instance had to move out of the area where the crime was committed, in lieu of prosecution and jail time.

Family secrets are private matters, but they can be written about at arm's-length in fiction, or by masking them cleverly in non-fiction.

As a writer, it might help to circle around the family secret and view it from multiple angles. Give the notorious act some depth, some facet or unexpected detail, so that your narrative transformation will lift it out of the realm of secrecy into art.

Exercise 12: Family Rewind

This exercise involves a great deal of imagination.

Think about your parents or your grandparents. Do you know where and how they met?

If so, take half a page to write down those details. Go directly to the source or check with someone who knows them, who can fill in the story.

Now comes the fun part:. Imagine that they never met. The scary part of this exercise is it means you would not exist, but that's not important right now.

If your parents or grandparents or aunt, uncle had never met, what paths might they have taken and who would they have become?

Write a four-page story speculating fully on those possibilities and then reunite them in a plausible situation.

For example, I know that my parents met in the music practice rooms in the Southern California college in the mid 1950s. My mom was already a talented composer and arranger. My dad did want to be at that college. He wanted to be at UCLA studying to be an engineer. He wanted to design sports cars. When my parents met and married and had two kids, they let go of their dreams.

What if my mom had not married my dad and taken her
composer skills to music studios in Los Angeles and ended
up as an arranger of 1960's pop songs? What if she ended up
living in Laurel Canyon with Joni Mitchell and Graham Nash,
married a music producer and eventually found herself raising
three kids in Malibu?

What if my dad followed his car design passion all the way to
Detroit, becoming the designer of a popular sports car
convertible. He remains single.

One time he is attending the Auto Show in Los Angeles and
on an afternoon off decides to drive up Pacific Coast Highway,
stopping at the Trancas market. A woman in the station wagon
backs into him and crumples the front bumper of his rental
car. They exchange insurance information.

He looks at her there in the Malibu sunlight and he wonders if
maybe he knew her in another life.

Exercise 13: Time Machine I

Get in the Time Machine. Go back two generations and choose a location where a grandparent has been. This can be indoors or outdoors. It could be a farmhouse, a factory, or a battlefield.

Take us there and describe the location from a cinematic viewpoint. Now tell us about the smells and the things we might taste. If it is a kitchen, this should be an easy task for you.

Now, have your grandparent pick up an object in the scene. What does it feel like to touch or use that object?

My grandfather Greyford (Grey) was a young father in the Depression, during the Great Depression without having any formal education.

Grey started out in the grocery business. When times were really tough in the 1930's,, he drove over the Grapevine from Los Angeles into the San Joaquin Valley and loaded his car with produce and poultry. I'm imagining he brought back live chickens, killed them at the house, dressed them and then took them back out for sale. He may have had a route of customers, or maybe he sold the food out of his car to passersby.

I'm not sure about all the details. I have few relatives left who can help me out, so I might resort to research or just use my imagination to figure it out.

Hopefully, this simple scene-setting exercise will help you explore the family member who is your character.

If it's easier, you can go back an additional generation to a great-grandparent. My great-great-father William was a barber on the super chief train between Chicago and Los Angeles. What was it like for him to hold a straight razor in his hand as the train raced over the rails, to shave a customer who was leaning back in the barber chair with such skill and safety?

See if you can find a similar situation in your family history.

Exercise 14: Time Machine II

Return to the Time Machine and pick an event from your childhood that you wish had gone differently.

In three to four pages, use your literary wizardry to make the outcome more to your liking.

Was a family member nearby or available? Could this family member have intervened?

Was a family member negligent or less-than-helpful in this incident?

Is it possible to establish redemption or forgiveness with them as you recreate the event?

As much as we would like our parents to be perfect, they weren't always able to ber supportive or have access to the resources to improve a difficult situation.

Make sure to render all the details of the childhood event, including recreating the sounds, smells, touch and taste associated with it. See if any new memories come to the surface during this exercise.

See if you can use your current wisdom to create a new perspective on the childhood event.

Further Reading

Dillard Annie, *The Writing Life*, 2013

Goldberg, Natalie, *Writing Down the Bones, Freeing the Writer Within*, 1986

Karr, Mary, *The Art of Memoir*, 2016

King, Steven, *On Writing - A Memoir of the Craft*, 2010

Anne Lamott, *Bird by Bird. Some Instructions on Writing in Life*, 1995

Maran Meredith, *Why We Write About Ourselves: Twenty Memoirists on Why They Expose Themselves (and Others) in the Name of Literature*, 2016

Obermeyer, Jon, *Brought into Light: The Making of Memoir*, 2018

Obermeyer, Jon, *Myriad: A Poet's Perspective on Writing*, 2017

Pressfield Stephen, *The War of Art: Break Through the Blocks and Win your Inner Creative Battles.* 2012

Zinsser, William, *On Writing Well: the informal guide to writing non-fiction*, 2006

About the Author

A native of Santa Barbara, California. Jon Obermeyer is a
graduate of Westmont College. He holds a Master of Fine Arts
in Creative Writing from the University of North Carolina
at Greensboro, where he earned a graduate fellowship and
served as associate poetry editor of *The Greensboro Review*.

Jon is the author of over twenty books of creative work, cover-
ing poetry, short stories, essays and memoir.

His short stories have appeared in *Equator, Cities & Roads,* and
O.Henry Festival Stories. In 1982, his short story "Not
Really Mine to Give" received runner up honors in the *Santa
Barbara News and Review* fiction contest. In 1986, novelist Clyde
Edgerton selected "Confessions of a Pacifist" as a finalist story
in the North Carolina Writers Network's fiction competition.

Jon has been a three-time finalist for the James Applewhite
Poetry Prize, sponsored by *North Carolina Literary Review.* His
poems have appeared in *The Greensboro Review, International
Poetry Review, Cobalt, A Carolina Literary Companion Spectrum.
Spectrum 60th anthology, Blue Pitcher, Coraddi, Phoenix, Santa
Barbara Magazine, Stroke Connection Magazine, Northern Virginia
Review,* and in the Greensboro anthology, *Edge of our World.*

His essays and book reviews have appeared in the *Greensboro
News & Review and The New York Times.*

He is retired and lives in Northern California.